touching air

gill shaw

Published in 2023 by
Stewed Rhubarb
Tarland, Aberdeenshire
www.stewedrhubarb.org

© 2023 Gill Shaw

The moral right of Gill Shaw to be identified
as author of this work has been asserted.

Editing by Angela Cleland

Printed & bound by Inky Little Fingers, UK

ISBN: 978-1-910416-27-3

'I reflect on our relationship through the lens of
wabi-sabi' was first published in *Gutter.*

'The observation of water' quotes 'The Trees' by Philip
Larkin, published in *The Complete Poems* (Faber & Faber)
and reprinted with permission.

For Luna:
for the tender moments
the exquisite kisses
and the gift of the pain
that brought the poetry.

Uisge beatha

You drink whisky. So, I want to learn
about whisky. Do you know the middle part
of the second distillation is called the heart?
Do you know the heart is the sweetest part?

Ethanol-filled, highly desirable, perfect
for whisky? If I were a gambling girl, I'd bet
this is the only love poem in the world
where the poet offers up the sweetest part

of the second distillation.
But I'm no gambler. Except
when I'm betting
on a sure thing.

And you are my sure thing.
Jigger me malted.
Jigger me nosed.
Jigger me rare.

Bring me the sweetness
of your second distillation.
Show me the acorn
of your ethanol

love.

The day you introduced me to your father

we sat on a bench that winked
steel through chipped burgundy
paint. You told me you liked
my shoes. We sat long. The sun

shone an unexpected ease, lit
golden flecks. I saw granite
stillness nod a blessing, heard
silence speak an affirmation.

I paused as we left, touched
two fingers to stone
and made him a promise

I didn't keep.

Senryū for Luna

#11
come, let's get lost in
the stacks of an old bookshop –
touch spines, steal kisses

#32
pass me my guitar
I'll play you country love songs
three chords and the truth

#237
take your forefinger
trace the lines of my tattoos
remind me to breathe

The angel's share

I bought my favourite scarf in a Bodrum boutique. White gossamer. Aegean blue angel wings. I gave you my favourite scarf so you could wear me round your neck. On the day you break my heart for the first time, you return it. My favourite scarf. My poetry books. Pink tissued, navy ribboned. With a card that tells me to "Stay Spellbinding". My favourite scarf smells of you. I lie   in the spot where you sat   on the day   our first kiss   danced in the glint   of your eye   and woke   from the flick   of your tongue   on your lip   before landing. I could tell you wanted to kiss me. It was written all over the upturned corners of your mouth. Not a smile. Not a pout. A moment. When your mouth

became want

became window

became wreathe.

My favourite scarf smells of you. I hold it to my face and breathe in the absence of you, distilled and carried on angel's wings. My whisky-barrel heart is still giving   you the angel's share. The smell of you lies heavy on my fingers again but not from the places I touched you, where my fingertips made dents. Holy,   unfillable   spaces   on the surface of your skin.

The smell of you still lies

heavy. My fingertips

are no longer mine.

They are gone.

They're with you.

They are still

leaving

dents on the surface

of your

skin.

Agape

AGREEMENT of the GROUNDS on which the AFFECTED
PARTIES shall ENGAGE ("AGAPE")
between
You ("the Loyalist")
and
Me ("the Lover")

WHEREAS
a) The parties acknowledge that they share a mutual
attraction to each other physically, emotionally,
intellectually and spiritually; and
b) The Loyalist wishes, subject to the terms set out
below, to maintain a platonic friendship (**"the
Friendship"**)

IT IS AGREED THAT

1. Definitions

"Afternoon Light" means
the period at or around 3pm each day when light indoors
begins to fade from its brightest, and is suffused with
a liminal quality, as can be particularly observed in
the seasons of autumn and winter.

"Commencement Date" means
the date of signature of AGAPE.

"Doing A Friday" means
any attempt by either party, in the latter part of any
week, to withdraw from communication with the other
party, indicate that they no longer wish to be party to
the Friendship, terminate the Friendship, or unfriend
the other party on Facebook.

"Pause Reality" means
the ability of the parties to free themselves from
the attachments, responsibilities, obligations and/or
loyalties in their day-to-day lives, for the purposes
of engaging in Romantic Communication and/or Beyond-
friendly Activity.

"Romantic Communication" means
the sending, by any electronic means, of messages,
memes, images, emojis, GIFS, quotes or other similar
electronic communications; and/or the oral communication
in person, by telephone or by electronic recording, of
any words which would ordinarily be exchanged between
individuals engaged in romantic or sexual relationships,
including any telephone calls made by the Loyalist to
the Lover at midnight requesting that she drive to her
to touch her skin. For the avoidance of doubt, Romantic
Communication includes describing any daydreams which
one party may have about the other, particularly where
any such daydreams involve Beyond-friendly Activity
which takes place during Afternoon Light.

"Beyond-friendly Activity" means
interactions between the parties which involve touching
skin; removing the other party's ring(s); holding hands;
interlacing fingers; smelling the other party's hair or
neck; resting or pressing limbs or other parts of the
body against the other party; kissing, licking, biting,
or sucking any part of the other party's person; the
insertion of any part of the body into any orifice of
the other party; removing items of the other party's
clothing; touching (through clothing) areas of the body
which would not ordinarily be touched by individuals in
a platonic relationship; and exchanging gifts of the
type that might be exchanged between romantic partners,
including but not limited to books of poetry, purple
alliums, garnet, and packets of Revels.

2. Duration of Agreement

AGAPE will commence on the Commencement Date and shall continue, subject to Clause 4, until terminated by The Loyalist.

3. Grounds of Engagement

3.1 The parties agree that they shall not:

    3.1.1 participate in Beyond-friendly Activity; or

    3.1.2 engage in Romantic Communication.

3.2 For the avoidance of doubt, nothing in AGAPE shall prevent the parties hugging in the way platonic friends ordinarily hug.

3.3 The parties shall use their best endeavours to avoid Doing A Friday.

4. Pausing Reality

4.1 Notwithstanding the provisions of Clause 3, the parties agree that they may, by mutual agreement, Pause Reality for the purposes of participating in Beyond-friendly Activity and/or Romantic Communication.

4.2 Any such agreement to Pause Reality shall not amount to a breach of AGAPE.

4.3 The parties agree that following the conclusion of any agreement to Pause Reality, they will not discuss any Beyond-friendly Activity which takes place and will refrain from any subsequent Romantic Communication relating to the Beyond-friendly Activity.

5. Breach of AGAPE

Where one party acts in breach of AGAPE, the innocent party may impose a penalty of their choosing. For the avoidance of doubt, any penalty imposed by the innocent party which amounts to Beyond-friendly Activity requires the agreement of the offending party.

6. Variation of AGAPE

The terms of AGAPE may be varied by the mutual agreement of the parties and recorded in writing.

7. Miscellaneous

In the event that, at any time, the Loyalist wishes to permanently Pause Reality, the Lover gives consent in perpetuity.

Signed _____

Date _____

The Loyalist

Signed _____

Date _____

The Lover

Pausing reality

Bring me your heels stinging,
nicked by marram swords.
Bring me the shingle that clings
between your toes.
Bring me the sand that dulls
the Go-Wild-erness on your toenails.
Bring me your salted shins.
Bring me your thighs
and the rise of their goosebumps.
Bring me your bathing suit, damp.
Bring me the sun,
curled in the waves
of your hair.
Bring me the heat
in the skin of your neck.
Bring me the gasp
escaped from your lips.
Bring me the pearl
of your teeth.
Bring me the upturned
corners of your mouth.
Bring me the shine
of your coconut shoulders
and let my fingertips
stick.

Kelpie

On the shore of Loch Ness our cantering   breath
set your garnet eyes ablaze. My fingers   waded
deep. The fire in your mane burned my   fingertips.

I held no   Luckenbooth.
You pulled me   under.
Drowned me and   swallowed

me whole.   Maybe
the iron in my   blood
might have saved   me.

But   you
didn't   break
the   skin.

To her supraclavicular fossa

I called her Luna in the moments when fingertip   words were all I could reach
with. She tethered me like the pull of the moon's gravity   on earth holds our planet in place.
Until I lost her to the ring on her finger and the gravity and the   good in her bones. The clavicle is the
only bone in the human body that lies horizontal. The bone that strains most to escape the orbits of muscle and sinew,
rising to arch its beauty. That afternoon, her clavicle arched for my tongue when I let it pause, crescented in the empty
hollow of you – her supraclavicular fossa. Her inhale of expectation cratered my tongue, phased it deeper into the
space of her like a lunar pull, ebbed in the tide of her rising shoulders. Tonight, my clavicle horizons rise in the waning
of her. Tears trace meridians, pool in my jugular notch, the feel of you under my tongue   / eclipsed.

- 15 -

How you might reflect on impelling me to kill

The first time she introduced me to her son
I gave him a yellow-potted sunflower. The perfect
gift for a budding horticulturalist.
Either side of the pot, he placed squat
toddler hands, lifted it high, carried it tall,
its sunflower head bobbing atop shirted leaves.

At the corner of the flowerbed, he knelt on leaves
strewn on the path. She crouched beside her son.
With them I felt sunflower tall.
When I crouched we made a perfect
trinity. Two radiant heliophiles squat
either side of the wee horticulturalist.

I am no horticulturalist.
My sleeve caught on the leaves
of a plant I didn't know. Squat,
coral flowers with palm-scalloped leaves. Her son
delighted in the colour of my pretty dress, *a perfect
match for the pretty flowers.* I felt sunflower tall.

Sunflowers need water, sunlight and strong roots to grow tall,
she said, loosening the plant from its pot – quite the horticulturalist.
Heads bowed, our triune trowels fashion the perfect
bed. She shook mud from the flower and leaves
and handed the rooted plant to her son.
Hands either side of the roots, in a toddler squat,

he bedded it, short and squat
in the ground. I unearthed her eyes. Said, *I hope it grows tall
for him.* Smiled. Shaded my eyes from the sun
silhouetting the fledgling horticulturalist,
standing sunflower tall. But I am the person that leaves.
And the sunflower didn't grow tall, it grew heads. Three perfect

heads, nine leaves. For silver-trailed slugs, the perfect
combination to whet their appetite, then sate their squat
bodies. She tried coffee grinds and copper wire to save the leaves
and the heads, wanted desperately to see them grow tall
for him. For me. She begged advice from a local horticulturalist,
plucked bloated slug corpses from beer-filled pots while her son

was climbing trees. I feel squat, not sunflower tall.
I am the person who leaves. I made her a murdering horticulturalist.
What a shining, perfect example to set for her son.

Shade: Rose Libertin

You

kiss properly.

I'll give you that.

Maybe danger roused

your mouth? Our last

kiss didn't announce

itself. A quick double

double : four chaste pecks in

a car park too peopled. I drove

home wearing your lipstick knowing

pink was never my colour

Confession

On the day you broke my heart
for the last time, I know
you meant to return

the garnet. You didn't.
You gave me back
the smoky quartz.

Our relationship as an assault of fencing with guilt and lust as your pair coaches

En garde

[PHASE 1]

Invitation. Advance.   Advance.   Engagement.   Touch.
Double touch. Derobement. Corps-a-corps. Thrust. Press. Volt.
                                                                Dis-
                                                                engage.

Bro   ken   t   ime.
         Forward recovery.   Advance.   Advance. Touch. Press.

Retreat.   Abstain.   No touch.
            Renewal.   Circle parry.
                             Reprise.
                                 Reprise.

[PHASE 2]

Renewal. Second intention. No touch. Abstain.
Advance. Engagement. Touch. Touch. Halt!
Forward recovery. Volt. Yielding parry. Touch. Flick. Touch. Halt!

Retreat.

Abstain. No touch.

Retreat.

[PHASE 3]

Change of engagement. No touch. Abstain.
Advance. Engagement. Ceding parry. Touch. Touch. Touch.

Retreat.

Attack. Riposte.

Counter time.

[BLACK CARD]

15 ways to stay alive

after Daphne Gottlieb

1. Cry. As often as you need to, so you don't drown from the inside.
2. Cast a binding spell to undo her magic.
3. Make an appointment for acupuncture. Let the acupuncturist read heartbreak on your tongue.
4. Eat. Even if all you eat is Mini Eggs.
5. Remember to breathe when her name is a sobbing climax.
6. Use your body as a billboard. Wear clothes that scream affirmations you don't believe in yet. *Love. Feeling Good. Today Is Going to Rock.*
7. Forget you wore the shirt that says *Today Is Going to Rock* on the day she kissed you for the first time. Forget she ever kissed you at all.
8. Pretend today really does *Rock.* Grab an air guitar. Keep your heart out of the mosh pit.
9. Buy a BFF bracelet for dry shampoo.
10. Take yourself to the movies. Wear a slash of red lipstick.
11. Try forest-bathing. Plant bare feet on the ground. Let blades of grass be the only blades that touch your skin.
12. Build a bomb shelter from oracle cards.
13. Forget there are Twin Flames.
14. Light a single flame to burn the card she sent you that told you to "Stay Spellbinding".
15. Stay Spellbinding.

The things that I am left with

after Ollie O'Neill

Theatre tickets. A tin of paint. Insomnia. The last drops in a department store sample of your favourite perfume. A print of the moon as it looked overhead on the night that we met. 5 unopened gifts, beautifully wrapped. A firm pillow on your side of the bed. A quarter bottle of Moonlight Magic. A length of navy ribbon. A Spotify subscription. 4 goodbye playlists. 9 songs I can't listen to. A craving for chocolate brownies. A flame-shaped stone that I picked off the beach. Lingerie with the tags still on. An envelope inked with my initial. A pair of Fit-Flops to wear when I bring in the washing. 367 senyrū. Used hankies in every pocket. Mascara stains on every pillowcase. 16 sets of oracle cards. 3 Tarot decks. Red spell candles. Clear quartz. Luna quartz. Smoky quartz. An empty wine bottle. A boarding pass. An unread book of poetry. A signed agreement. A packet of Revels. Autumn in a vase. A 3-inch scar. 4 skipping stones. A page torn from a notebook – *I do love you.*

(Untitled poem which makes it into my pamphlet
after my doctor writes to my publisher to advise that
allowing me to use a hyphen in a nonet would be a
reasonable adjustment)

Today I know that I am healing:
for the first time since you left me
I wrote a poem that is
not a list poem. There's
no figurative
language but it
is in po-
etic
form.

I try to write a poem using a homonym but I can't stop thinking about kissing you

I don't know how to kiss lightly.
I don't mean / the measure / of pressure / I bring to a kiss /
    with my lips.
I don't know / how to kiss / lightly.
I don't know / how to come / to a kiss / with my lips /
    where my lips / are not all of me.

When I kiss / I bring all of me.

I miss / the weight / of your kisses. The bruises they left /
    on my lips.
You don't kiss / lightly.

I don't / know / how / to / kiss / lightly.
If I can't
kiss / lightly
and
kiss / lightly
how / will I ever kiss / anyone
other
than you.

The observation of water

The trees are coming into leaf
Like something almost being said;
The recent buds relax and spread,
Their greenness is a kind of grief.
  – Philip Larkin, *The Trees*

Spring slithers in like lithium snaking
through veins, lifting the depression
of winter. In its wake snowdrops hang
weary heads. Crocuses
swarm. Nature sings
a siren song I answer.
I keep coming upon bodies.
So many bodies of water. Benches
by beaches, by riverbanks, by lochans.
The trees are coming into leaf:

growth unfurls in stillness.
Stillness gives water
a voice. Urges it to speak up.
I listen for the gasps of waves
on empty shores, listen
for the whispers of rivers
writhing along pebbled paths.
I search for the truth held in the open
mouths of bodies of water
like something almost being said.

I sit on benches with the echo
of our conversations. The air
screams your absence.
I wonder if you sit with her
on any of these benches. The screaming
air stills. Silent bodies
of water hold their truth in open
mouths. Branches stretch. Breathe.
Growth unfurls in stillness,
the recent buds relax and spread

their leafy wings. Leaves take to the air
like dancers taking to the floor.
Waltzing to the gasps of waves, the whispers
of rivers, the truth held in the open
mouths of bodies of water:
that Summer's tender dance will always lead
to Autumn's fall. I toe the blades
of grass at my feet. My ribs still
cage my emerald jealousies.
Their greenness is a kind of grief.

Conversations with my 4-year-old

i) He talks about the weather, using the sun and rain as metaphors for my joy and sadness

It's not supposed to be rainy.

It's supposed to be shiny with sun.

Maybe the rain and the sun had a race and the rain got here first.

ii) He asks about playlists, using extended metaphor to call out my willingness to allow you to repeatedly break my heart

*Mama, if you put a song on repeat will it play over
and over and
over and
over?*

iii) He shows off his bath-crayon picture, using personification to make you a rainbow-coloured beach

Mama, do you really love the rainbow-coloured beach?

It's a shame there isn't a rainbow-coloured beach around here.

I reflect on our relationship through
the lens of wabi-sabi

In
late
May
cherry
blossoms
strew the pave-
ment. Their petals
are tiny pink tears. The
flattened edges curl and
rip and brown. Never
was an ending wept
so tenderly.

Postscript

I'm still finding strawberry stars
stellared from an unlidded blender
glistening in the crevices of my kitchen.
I'm still painting my toenails
with Moonlight Magic.
I'm still resting my forehead on the fridge
that caught your back.
I'm still listening to your playlists.
I'm still giving you the angel's share.
I'm still searching for you in every sunset.
I'm still waiting for your midnight call.
I'm still hoping you'll pause reality.
I'm still longing to see the upturned corners
of your mouth.
I'm still watching the language of you
fall onto every blank page.
I'm still unable to kiss
the inside
of anyone else's wrist.
I'm still reaching with fingertip words.
I'm still touching
air.

Notes

Uisge beatha is Scots Gaelic for whisky, literally 'water of life'.

The phrase three chords and the truth is from the 2018 movie *Wild Rose*, written by Nicole Taylor.

Agape is the highest form of love: transcendent and unconditional.

Marram is the dense, prickly grass you find growing in sand dunes.

A luckenbooth is a Scottish brooch, usually depicting a crowned heart or two intertwined hearts, often given as a betrothal gift or love token in the 17th century. I learned about luckenbooths from Jenni Fagan's 2021 novel *Luckenbooth*.

The supraclavicular fossa is the name of the indentation immediately above the clavicle (or collarbone), which appears when you shrug your shoulders.

Garnet is the stone of commitment.

Smoky quartz helps provide clarity, clear negativity and remove challenging obstacles.

Binding spells are cast to limit a witch's magic, and I read about them in the *All Souls Trilogy* book series by Deborah Harkness.

Twin flames are defined by writer Kate Rose in her 2020 book *You Only Fall in Love Three Times* as "highly connected spiritual relationships, the kind of love we often refer to when we speak about meeting our other half".

Wabi-sabi is the Japanese concept of finding beauty in the imperfect and impermanent.

Stewed Rhubarb is Charlie Roy and Duncan Lockerbie.
We are a small, inclusive and independent Scottish press
that champions new and diverse poetry.

www.stewedrhubarb.org

STEWED RHUBARB